KRISTINA RUTHERFORD

– LEVEL THE – PLAYING FIELD

THE PAST, PRESENT, AND FUTURE OF WOMEN'S PRO SPORTS

FOR CHARLEY, AVA, AND QUINNE

KRISTINA RUTHERFORD

OWLKIDS BOOKS

— LEVEL THE —
PLAYING FIELD

THE PAST, PRESENT, AND FUTURE OF WOMEN'S PRO SPORTS

Text © 2016 Kristina Rutherford

Photo Credits: ©Tribune Content Agency LLC/Alamy: 7; ©Charles Platiau/Reuters: 8, left; ©Mike Blake/Reuters: 10; ©2015 Canadian Olympic Committee: 12; Public domain: 13, left; Jerry Cooke/Sports Illustrated/Getty Images: 14; ©Shaun Best/Reuters: 15, left; Nathaniel S. Butler/NBAE via Getty Images: 15, right; Jeff Bottari/Zuffa LLC via Getty Images: 16, left; ©Mike Blake/Reuters: 16, right; ©USA Today Sports/Reuters: 18; ©Jonathan Larsen/Diadem Images/Alamy: 21, right; ©Getty Images: 23; ©Tribune Content Agency LLC/Alamy: 24; ©Tami Chappell/Reuters: 25, bottom left; ©Cal Sport Media/Alamy: 28; Brian Babineau/NBAE via Getty Images: 30; © Ken Hawkins/ZUMA Press Inc./Alamy: 31, left; ©Toby Melville/Reuters: 32; © Brian Snyder/Reuters: 33, left; ©Mark J. Rebilas-USA TODAY Sports/Reuters: 34, left; ©Brian Babineau/NBAE via Getty Images: 35, right; ©Anne-Marie Sorvin/USA Today Sports/Reuters: 36, left; © Lucas Jackson/Reuters: 36, right; Olivier Morin/AFP/Getty Images: 41, left; ©Mike Blake/Reuters: 41, right; ©Reuters Photographer: 42; ©Michael Chow/USA TODAY Sports: 43; ©Evan Habeeb/USA TODAY Sports/Reuters: 44, left; Derick E. Hingle/USA TODAY Sports/Reuters: 44, right; John Dorton/www.isiphotos.com: 46; ©EPA Agency B.V./Alamy: 48; ©Lucy Nicholson/Reuters: 49, left; ©Mohamad Dabbouss/Reuters: 49, right; David Price/Arsenal FC via Getty Images: 50, left; ©Mike Segar/Reuters: 50, right; Jennifer S. Altman/Contour via Getty Images: 51, left; Linda Cataffo/NY Daily News Archive via Getty Images: 51, right; ©Reuters Staff/Reuters: 53; © Debby Wong/Shutterstock.com: back cover, bottom far left; © Iurii Osadchi/Shutterstock.com: back cover, bottom, second from left; all other photos royalty-free (Dreamstime, Shutterstock)

Owlkids Books acknowledges the financial support of the Canada Council for the Arts, the Ontario Arts Council, the Government of Canada through the Canada Book Fund (CBF) and the Government of Ontario through the Ontario Media Development Corporation's Book Initiative for our publishing activities.

Published in Canada by
Owlkids Books Inc.
10 Lower Spadina Avenue
Toronto, ON M5V 2Z2

Published in the United States by
Owlkids Books Inc.
1700 Fourth Street
Berkeley, CA 94710

Library and Archives Canada Cataloguing in Publication

Rutherford, Kristina, author
      Level the playing field : the past, present, and future of women's pro sports / Kristina Rutherford.

Includes bibliographical references and index.
ISBN 978-1-77147-160-2 (hardback)

     1. Sports for women--Juvenile literature. 2. Professional sports-- Juvenile literature. I. Title.

GV709.R88 2016   j796.082   C2015-908028-2

Library of Congress Control Number: 2016930941

Edited by: John Crossingham
Designed by: Alisa Baldwin

ONTARIO ARTS COUNCIL
CONSEIL DES ARTS DE L'ONTARIO
an Ontario government agency
un organisme du gouvernement de l'Ontario

Canada Council   Conseil des Arts
for the Arts   du Canada

Canadä

Manufactured in Dongguan, China, in July 2016, by Toppan Leefung Packaging & Printing (Dongguan) Co., Ltd.
Job # BAYDC22

A   B   C   D   E   F

Publisher of Chirp, chickaDEE and OWL
www.owlkidsbooks.com | Owlkids Books is a division of    Bayard
CANADA

CONTENTS

ON A FIRST-NAME BASIS

A famous athlete like LeBron James needs no introduction, right? Because, well, he's LeBron James. It helps that he's six foot eight and you can't possibly miss him. We know LeBron because of what he can do on a basketball court. Because he has been named Most Valuable Player (MVP) in the National Basketball Association (NBA) four times. LeBron has more than a dozen different pairs of shoes named after him and more than eight million followers on Instagram.

Then there's Maya. She was a No. 1 overall pick in the Women's National Basketball Association (WNBA) and won the championship title her rookie year. Like LeBron, she was named MVP in her league. Before that, Maya led the University of Connecticut to back-to-back national titles— and undefeated seasons. Maya is an Olympic gold medalist and a multiple-time WNBA All-Star.

And yet, Maya enjoys only a small fraction of the fame and celebrity that LeBron does. She earns almost nothing compared with what LeBron makes. And she *needs* an introduction: She's Maya Moore.

But why is that? Why is the pro sports experience so different for a man versus a woman? Why aren't athletes like LeBron and Maya valued and recognized equally for their talent?

Some of the world's biggest star athletes are going to help us tackle this subject. Like Caroline Wozniacki, the first Scandinavian woman to hold the World No. 1 tennis ranking. Golfer Inbee Park, a multiple-time major winner on the LPGA Tour. Danica Patrick, the most successful female race car driver in history. We'll hear from Olympic gold medalists, world champions, and sports legends.

What they all agree on is this: We are looking at the most potential-filled point in history for women in pro sports. The opportunities are bigger than they've ever been, and they're growing. And the thing is, you have a role in this, too. The advancements we're seeing start with kids like you. They happen in schoolyards like yours and gain momentum in gyms like the one you play in.

And so one day, a female basketball player with Maya Moore's skill will need no introduction. She'll just be Maya.

Maya Moore of the Minnesota Lynx accepts the 2014 WNBA MVP award.

CHAPTER 1

LET'S TALK
PROGRESS

Have you ever wanted to try something really badly but not been given the chance? Maybe you want to act in a play, but your school doesn't have a drama program. You have the desire but not the opportunity. It's frustrating, isn't it?

That right there—a lack of opportunity—is among the biggest reasons women's pro sports are behind men's in so many ways. For a long time, girls and women simply didn't get a turn. They didn't have teams to play for or championship games to aspire to.

If you're a soccer player, imagine that your school doesn't have a team for girls, and your town or city doesn't have a club team for girls your age. Imagine it doesn't have a team for girls any age, period. That was once the reality.

This may seem hard to believe today. After all, we see plenty of examples of talented professional female athletes performing on the biggest stages in sport. Michelle Wie drains a long birdie putt and fiercely pumps her fist, minutes before she hoists the U.S. Open trophy. Maria Sharapova drops to her knees on the tennis court and screams with joy after winning the fifth major championship of her career. Saki Kumagai converts on a penalty kick, then throws up her arms as she and her teammates celebrate Japan's first-ever World Cup win. All these moments were witnessed and celebrated by millions of people around the world.

Not only that, but today a female athlete can also be selected in a professional sports draft. She can be inducted into halls of fame alongside fellow athletes like Michael Jordan and Wayne Gretzky. You might see her face on a cereal box or buy her basketball shoe or wear a jersey with her name and number on it. Today, if you're a girl playing hockey or if tennis is your passion, there is a chance that one day you can play professionally. And maybe that's what you're telling your friends you want to do.

But it wasn't long ago that none of this was happening. It might surprise you how much the landscape of women's pro sports has changed and how fast. Even since your very first day of school (remember kindergarten?) so much has changed for sportswomen. It's changed even more since your parents were born, not to mention your grandparents.

Consider that only 30 years ago, a soccer talent like American star Alex Morgan may have gone undiscovered simply because she didn't have a professional league to strive for or a female sports role model to look up to. A talent like Alex might never have developed those skills on the field in the first place.

How come?

Women didn't have the opportunity.

LEFT: Japanese National Team star Saki Kumagai.
RIGHT: Maria Sharapova of Russia clobbers a return.

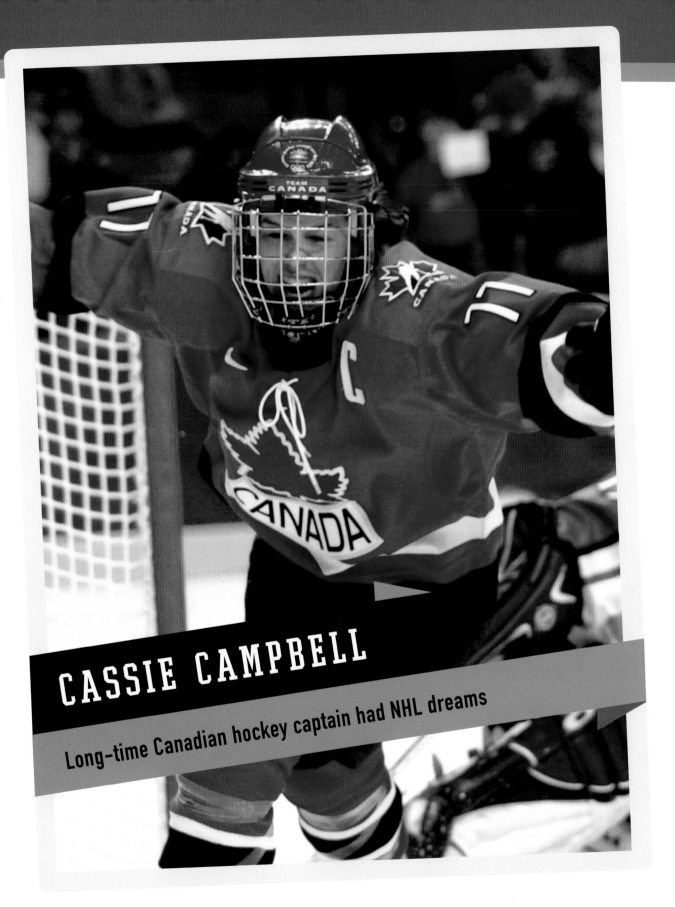

CASSIE CAMPBELL

Long-time Canadian hockey captain had NHL dreams

Cassie Campbell drops her stick on the ice, whips her gloves off, and skates—full tilt—at her teammate, Canadian goalie Kim St-Pierre. Cassie hollers "Woo!" as she skates, and she's airborne as soon as she gets to the goal crease, throwing herself into a pileup that's formed on top of Kim. It's that classic sports celebration, where you jump on your teammates because you're *that* excited. Canada beat the rival Americans in the women's hockey gold medal final at the 2002 Olympics, hence the jumping and yelling and fist pumps.

In a career that includes six World Championships and two Olympic gold medals, this is Cassie's highlight. Even looking back on all those moments, Cassie still thinks this particular one is "crazy." Because as a little girl growing up in the 1970s—that might be around the same time your mom or dad grew up—she never dreamed she'd have a chance to accomplish any of this in hockey.

Q: HOW DID YOU GET INTO ICE HOCKEY?

CASSIE: I fought my parents: "Let me play!" They put me in figure skating, the typical girl thing. But my brother had a girl on his hockey team, Jennifer Minkus. I came up with this brilliant idea of saying to them, "Well, Jennifer Minkus plays!" That next year I started playing on a boys' team. I was six. I had a short little haircut, so my first year the boys didn't even know I was a girl until we had a swimming party at the end of the season. The other kids were asking, "Why are you wearing that bathing suit?" Then they realized, "Oh my god—she's a girl!"

Q: THAT'S SO FUNNY. WAS IT SEEN AS "WEIRD" TO BE A GIRL WHO PLAYED HOCKEY IN THE LATE 1970s AND EARLY 1980s?

CASSIE: I don't think it was as taboo as playing in my mother's generation, but you walked into the rink and you heard the whispering and people saying, "The girl shouldn't play." You heard the naysayers, but you played because you loved it.

Q: WHAT WERE YOUR HOCKEY DREAMS AS A YOUNG KID?

CASSIE: I looked to the National Hockey League [NHL] as a possibility because that's all I knew. I didn't know any female role models as far as hockey players went. It wasn't until 1990 that we had the first Women's World Championships, where I finally got introduced to people like Angela James and Geraldine Heaney. In 1992, we found out women's hockey was going to be at the 1998 Olympics. I was really lucky because the game evolved over my career.

Q: WHAT WAS IT LIKE TO PLAY IN THE FIRST OLYMPICS TO INCLUDE WOMEN'S HOCKEY?

CASSIE: To be on that stage, to be accepted—it was incredible. The NHL players were coming to our games. It was a really exciting time.

Q: WHAT DO YOU THINK WHEN YOU LOOK AT THE WOMEN'S GAME TODAY?

CASSIE: One of the best nights of my life was in 2010, watching the first two women, Angela James and Cammi Granato, be inducted into the Hockey Hall of Fame. Look how far we've come. There are so many more options for girls now. They can grow up wanting to become whatever they want, and that was something that wasn't around when I was growing up. And I'm not even that old, you know?

OPPORTUNITY KNOCKS

There was no "poof!" moment for female athletes—they didn't wake up with a chance to suddenly play pro sports or win an Olympic medal. The movement for women's acceptance in sport has taken a lot of time and work.

But what got the movement going in the first place? Where did these opportunities come from? Let's take a look at some early kick-starters.

THE WOMEN AT HOME

Sometimes, an event can be so big that it changes the way an entire society thinks in unpredictable ways. World War I (1914–18) and World War II (1939–45) both had this effect, changing everything from industry and scientific innovation to politics and women's rights. At the time, only men really fought in the armies of the world. The soldiers that went off to fight in those devastating conflicts left their countries behind, as well as their daughters, sisters, mothers, and wives.

Even during wars as devastating as those, countries couldn't stand still. And so women took up many jobs previously held only by men. And they did them well. The confidence gained during that time gave women the feeling that they could do more than the jobs they were usually allowed, like teaching. They felt empowered. They knew that they could work alongside men to everyone's benefit.

And they pushed for further participation in sports, too.

HIGHER, FASTER, STRONGER

By the 1920s—after World War I ended—women were competing in eight events at the Olympic Games, including archery and athletics. If this number sounds small, it was actually major progress—female athletes hadn't even been allowed to compete in the first-ever Olympics in 1896. Can you imagine that? Back then, many people believed sport would make a woman less feminine or even damage her reproductive system. They worried what might happen to her body if she ran farther than 800 meters.

But with women taking on bigger roles in society during wartime, minds started to change. Women could do what many previously thought impossible. Growing participation in the Olympic program is just one example of this societal shift.

AMERICA'S GAME CHANGER

Getting to compete in the Olympics was one thing. Developing athletes—or training them to perform at their best on these stages—was a whole other story.

TOP LEFT: Female Olympians from 1924. Women competed in every Olympic discipline for the first time in 2012. TOP MIDDLE: Senator Birch Bayh runs with female athletes at Purdue University, circa 1972. TOP RIGHT: Girls high school basketball got a big boost from Title IX.

Women needed leagues and structures so they could compete and improve their skills in the four years between each Olympics.

An American law from the 1970s went a long way in providing just that. It had a big hand in increasing opportunity for female athletes. Before this law was passed, a speedy female runner couldn't have her college tuition paid for her like she can today. Women couldn't get athletic scholarships. And intercollegiate sports, the way your school plays against other schools? At most schools, that existed only for boys...until Title IX.

This law was introduced in 1972 by Indiana Senator Birch Bayh. Interestingly, his concern wasn't just athletics. He proposed the law so that "no person in the United States shall, on the basis of sex, be excluded from participation in, [or] be denied the benefits of...any education program or activity receiving federal financial assistance." In other words, equal rights and opportunities for women at schools. But as far as any law's impact on women's sport goes, there has never been anything like it.

THE TITLE IX OLYMPICS

Title IX required American schools to spend equally on men and women's sports. That was enormous: Some colleges had used less than 1 percent of their athletic budget on women. The law forced schools to make drastic changes. And so, women's college teams started popping up all over the U.S.

BY THE NUMBERS

The most immediate result of Title IX? It got girls playing. The year it was passed, 294,015 American girls played high school sports. Two years later, the number nearly quintupled to 1.3 million. Dr. Nancy Lough is a professor who specializes in women's sport research at University of Nevada, Las Vegas (UNLV). She says the result of Title IX is simple: "The U.S. is far ahead of other countries in participation in sport among girls."

By the 1996 Olympics, many girls who had benefited from Title IX's changes had now become world-class athletes. The American women stole the show. And the American public saw the result of Title IX in the form of gold medals in soccer, basketball, gymnastics, swimming...you get the picture.

SHE'S THE KING

There are many reasons for the progress we've seen in women's pro sports. Civil rights movements, new laws, even wars—these things all change a society. But this progress is also made up of individuals who fought for equality.

And perhaps no single person has had a bigger impact than Billie Jean King. Remember that name: Billie Jean is to women's sport what Michael Jackson is to pop music.

Using a tennis racket and a court as her stage, the six-time Wimbledon champion waged one of the most significant battles across sport and society. She taught the world it's more than OK for a woman to be a jock: It's worth celebrating.

KING OF A MOVEMENT

In Billie Jean's day, women made a fraction of what men made on the pro tennis tour. But she fought for equal pay for women, and she helped cofound the Women's Tennis Association (WTA), which is now home to some of the most successful female athletes in the world. "Tennis has always been reserved for the rich, the white, the males," Billie Jean said, back in 1973. "And I've always pledged to change all that."

A former World No. 1 on the WTA Rankings, Denmark's Caroline Wozniacki is just one of the hundreds of players benefiting from what Billie Jean helped start. "Billie Jean fought for our right to play and play equally," Caroline says. "Not only did she prove herself as an athlete, but she stood up against the world of tennis. She's an inspiration to stand up for what you believe in."

THE BATTLE OF THE SEXES

Billie Jean's most impactful moment from a social standpoint was a single match. Imagine this scene, if you can: It's 1973, and 29-year-old Billie Jean is challenged to a match by a retired 55-year-old former male pro named Bobby Riggs. The duel is called the Battle of the Sexes, and it's exactly that:

TOP LEFT: Billie Jean King hoists her trophy after beating Bobby Riggs in the Battle of the Sexes match. TOP MIDDLE: Billie Jean with Serena and Venus Williams. BOTTOM RIGHT: Former NBA Commissioner David Stern at an event to support the WNBA.

man versus woman. In the lead-up, Bobby says things like: "I'll tell you why I'll win. She's a woman, and they don't have any emotional stability." Bobby said a lot worse, too. It would make you cringe. But his chauvinism only increased the hype to make this the most-watched tennis match the world had yet seen.

More than 50 million people tuned in to watch Billie Jean make a statement for the ages: She beat Bobby in straight sets, 6–4, 6–3, 6–3. It was monumental because it was about more than tennis. Hers was a win for women everywhere: Women fighting for equality at work, at school, at home, you name it. "I thought it would set us back 50 years if I didn't win that match," Billie Jean said afterward. "It would ruin the women's tour and affect all women's self-esteem."

Billie Jean also helped push against another significant barrier in sports—prejudice against gay athletes. As one of the first-ever high-profile openly gay athletes, Billie Jean blazed a trail for others to feel open and comfortable with their identity in the public eye. Jason Collins, the first openly gay player in the NBA, thanked her specifically after he decided to come out to the public in 2013. Billie Jean's reach across society has been enormous.

WHEN MEN ADD THEIR VOICE

Those who battle for women's rights in sport aren't always women. Just as it was a male senator who introduced Title IX, a male golf coach from the University of Miami, Norm Parsons, pushed to award the first-ever sport scholarship to a woman because, as he said, "It was the right thing to do." (And his team then won back-to-back national championships. Doing the right thing paid off.)

Among the biggest supporters of the WNBA is former NBA commissioner David Stern. And among the biggest supporters of the Canadian Women's Hockey League (CWHL) in North America is Brian Burke, a long-time NHL executive.

Men and women, boys and girls: The fight for equality in sport is at its best when it, too, is handled equally.

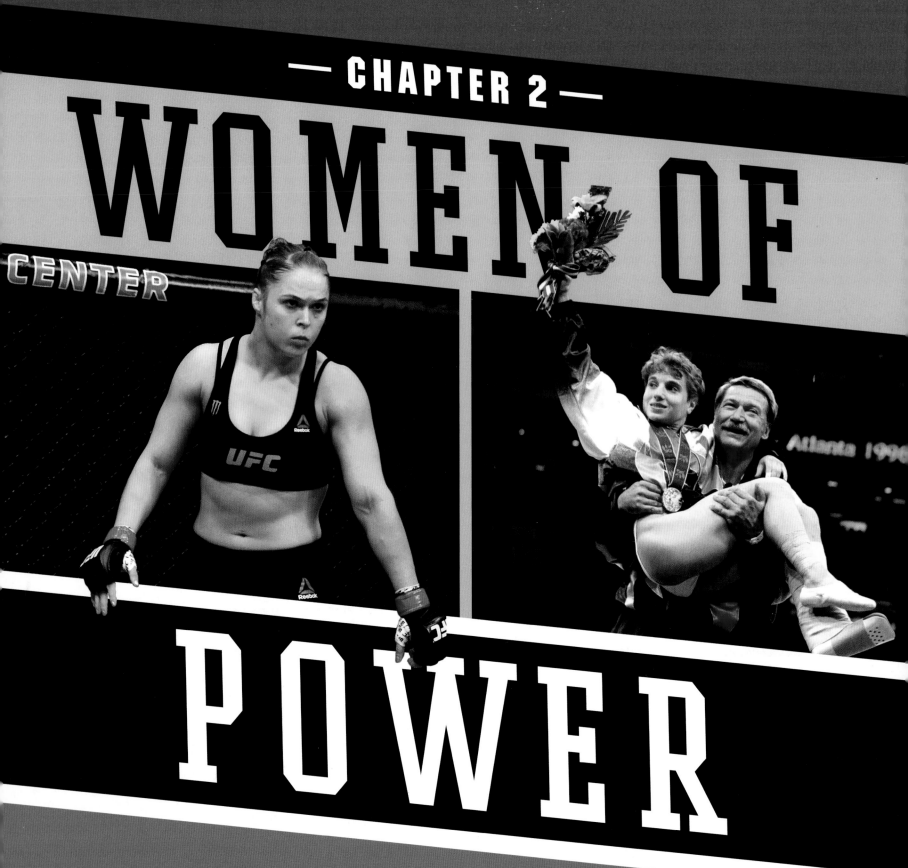

CHAPTER 2

WOMEN OF POWER

CENTER

We are inundated on a daily basis with images of women. Many are the beautiful faces you see promoting products like jeans and shampoo and nail polish. Others are in the public eye because they have an artistic talent like singing or acting. Some of these people use their celebrity to challenge ideas of what a woman is or should be. But it's female athletes who most consistently give us representations of women who embody qualities like toughness and power and tenacity. These are the famous women who use their strength and physicality to earn a living.

That's big, if you really think about it. Because for a very long time, a woman's role in society was viewed as little more than being feminine and well-mannered and providing for her family: cooking, cleaning, and taking care of the kids. She had to be ladylike. Playing sports? That was unladylike. But what it means to be a lady has changed. And *is* changing. Dramatically.

As we'll see here, female athletes today still have to overcome stereotypes. They're criticized for being too muscular. Or being just a pretty face. Or even accused that their participation in sport is nothing more than a marketing ploy, that they don't really have the strength and natural ability to play as well as men. The number of women who are proving those stereotypes wrong, however, is growing.

What's more, we don't find these groundbreaking athletes competing only in traditionally rough, aggressive sports like football and hockey and mixed martial arts (MMA). We find them figure skating and doing gymnastics, too. In fact, a four-foot-nine, 87-pound American gymnast named Kerri Strug is responsible for one of the gutsiest performances—by anyone—ever. At the 1996 Olympics, Kerri not only landed an incredible routine off the vault, but she did it with a sprained ankle and torn ligaments. In fact, she stuck the landing—coming down with her full force and power—*on* that injured ankle. *Thud.* Then, she lifted up her injured left leg, winced in pain, saluted the judges, and celebrated. Her landing meant the Americans had won Olympic gold in the team event. And then finally, Kerri fell to the floor in pain. Her coach carried her to the podium so she could receive her medal.

Moments like that one, witnessed by millions worldwide, get people to think differently about what female athletes are capable of. U.S. gymnastics coach Béla Károlyi captured it best, after Kerri's performance: "People think these girls are fragile dolls. They're not. They're courageous."

And let's add another word to that: powerful. Much of what female athletes struggle against is the perception that they can't be as powerful as men. Perhaps it's worth hearing from a woman dedicated to becoming as powerful as she can be.

LEFT: MMA star Ronda Rousey.
RIGHT: Kerri Strug and her coach, Béla Károlyi.

17

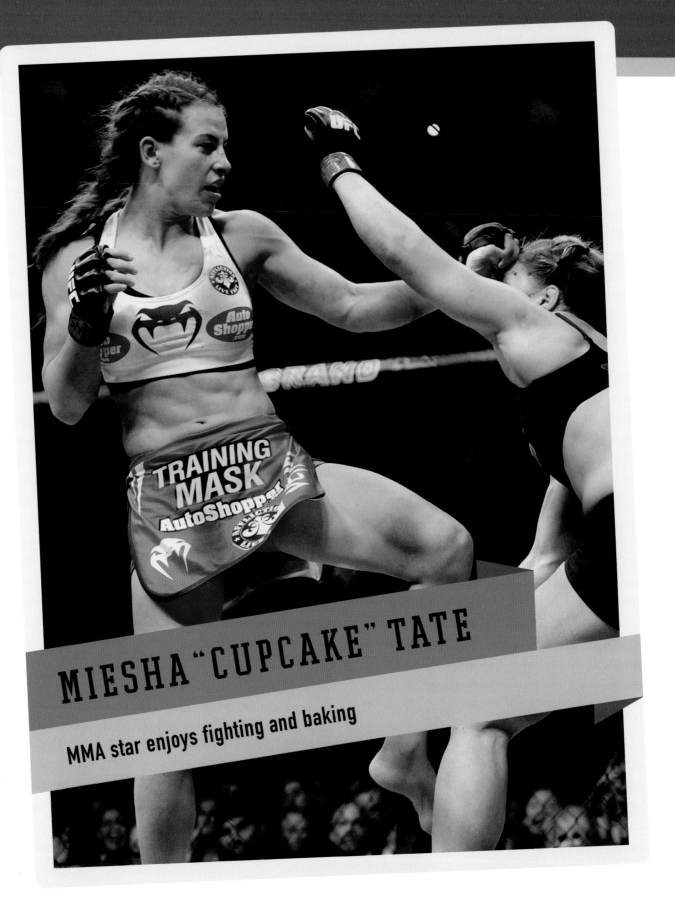

MIESHA "CUPCAKE" TATE

MMA star enjoys fighting and baking

Miesha Tate stands inside an octagon-shaped ring and waits for the referee to signal the start of this fight. The eight walls that surround her are made of metal chain-link fencing, like that which might border your schoolyard. Miesha wears padded black gloves on her hands because she's an MMA fighter. That means she throws punches like a boxer, takes down opponents like a martial artist, and grapples like a wrestler. Even kicking is allowed in her sport.

Miesha's nickname is Cupcake. Her long brown hair is pulled back into two braids. By the fourth round of this fight, Miesha has won again. She loosens her hold on her opponent and falls to the mat smiling, hands over her face. The crowd is going ballistic—picture your school's auditorium, filled with screaming students. Now double the noise and excitement, and then double it again. It's all for Miesha.

In a sport known for aggression and blood and broken bones, Miesha is among the very best in the world—on March 6, 2016, she defeated Holly Holm to become the UFC Women's Bantamweight Champion.

Q: YOU'VE SAID THAT YOUR JOB IS EMPOWERING. WHAT DO YOU MEAN BY THAT?

MIESHA: The career that I've picked, it's not an easy one or an accepted one for a female to pursue, especially when I first started. But I believe that if you choose a profession that other people deem as not really meant for men or meant for women, it shouldn't matter. Do what makes you happy.

Q: DO YOU STILL GET THE FEELING THAT SOME PEOPLE BELIEVE IT'S NOT ACCEPTABLE FOR A GIRL TO WANT TO FIGHT?

MIESHA: Yes. I still get strange reactions when I tell people what I do. I travel a lot for MMA, and I'll be sitting next to someone on an airplane who is not familiar with me or with my sport. We get talking about what we do for work. I usually try to ease them into it. I start out by saying, "I'm a professional athlete," and they usually say, "Oh, are you a gymnast?" I'm like, "No, I'm a fighter." Then their jaw drops, and they don't know what to say. I explain everything. It's very foreign, the idea that women would get into a cage and want to fight each other. Some people think it's great, and others are like, "What? Why would you want to do that? Isn't that dangerous? Don't you worry about your face?" They have all these worries for me.

Q: SOME PEOPLE EVEN SAY YOU'RE TOO PRETTY TO FIGHT. WHAT DO YOU SAY TO THAT?

MIESHA: (*Laughs*). I don't think that's a valid point. Looks have nothing to do with who you are on the inside and what drives you. I can't help it if it bothers them that my profession is a full-contact sport. [It's that] good old saying, you don't judge a book by its cover.

Q: HOW'D YOU GET YOUR NICKNAME, CUPCAKE?

MIESHA: When I started my career [in 2007], girls would call me out and want to fight me because they thought I was a cupcake—in other words, that I wasn't tough. They thought, "How can she wear a dress and heels and do her makeup and look girly and be a good fighter? I will smash this girl." It used to really anger me. Like, really? "OK, wait 'til I get these heels and this dress off!" (*Laughs*). If you want to underestimate me because I'm girly, be my guest. Call me Cupcake. It's a funny twist on the whole thing. Also, I love cupcakes and baking.

SO UNSTEREO- TYPICAL

A stereotype is a widely held perception about something or someone. We all encounter stereotypes in our lives. It's like assuming the kid in your class who's a math genius is a nerd who studies nonstop. At least, that's the stereotype. Except, surprise! He's also the star receiver on the school's football team. Wait: A smart jock? How can that be? Easy. People are capable of many things.

Many stereotypes focus on a person's gender as the thing that determines what they can—and can't—do. So what about a male nurse? A female president? People in these roles all challenge conventional thought, simply because their jobs were held by members of the opposite sex in the past. Because she fights for a living, Miesha Tate is breaking a stereotype. She's challenging the idea that women don't fight, that they're too fragile or afraid to get hurt. She's challenging the idea that women aren't tough. She contradicts these perceptions every time she steps into a cage for a bout.

BUCKING THE TREND

In pro sports, we are seeing more and more women breaking into roles that are considered "male" or "masculine" and crushing gender stereotypes in the process. And thanks to this, there are more athletic opportunities today for women than ever before.

Have you ever heard people say that women make bad drivers? (Yes, that's another stereotype!) Danica Patrick puts that theory to shame. Danica is a professional race car driver and the most successful woman ever in American open-wheel racing. She races almost exclusively against men—and she's the only woman ever to win an IndyCar Series race.

Danica also models and has so many endorsements that she's one of the most recognizable race car drivers in the world. But she wouldn't be had she not broken into the male-dominated world of race car driving. "I feel very lucky to be able to do what I do," Danica says. "Every now and again you pause for a second and realize the things that you do and the people that you meet and the places that you go and the experiences that you have are pretty awesome."

ABOVE: Indy car driver Danica Patrick. MIDDLE: Patrick's car mid-race. RIGHT: Brazilian soccer star Marta.

DON'T SWEAT, DON'T GET DIRTY...JUST KIDDING

In the late 1800s, golf and croquet were some of the first organized sports deemed acceptable for women. Why? Because they were the least physical. According to the prevailing thought of the day, a woman's anatomy couldn't handle rough sports like football and hockey. But as much as attitudes have changed—please roughhouse, sweat, and get very dirty—archaic thinking still lingers. Before women's ski jumping gained inclusion on the Olympic program in 2014, some officials involved with the sport said they believed jumping would harm women's reproductive systems—despite a lack of evidence.

THE FEMALE PELÉ

As difficult as these stereotypes have been to break in North America, breaking into sport as a woman in Brazil poses even more of a challenge. In that South American country, a law even stood from 1941 to 1979 that prohibited women and girls from playing most sports. Imagine that: All girls could do was watch.

But thankfully, a young Brazilian girl named Marta Vieira da Silva challenged conventional thought. Marta started dribbling soccer balls in the 1980s—although this was after the law had fallen, it was still at a time when women weren't encouraged to be athletic. The boys she played soccer with on the streets often made fun of Marta.

They don't make fun of her anymore. Marta has since led Brazil to two Olympic silver medals and earned the nickname "the female Pelé." It's a high compliment, since Pelé may be the best soccer player ever to play the game. But Marta did something even Pelé never did: She won five straight World Player of the Year awards from the Fédération Internationale de Football Association (FIFA). That's a record.

THE EVOLUTION OF STRENGTH

All athletes—male and female—continue to push the boundaries of what we think is humanly possible. Part of this comes down to the desire of the athlete. Part of it is natural talent—some people are born athletic. But overall, today's athletes are stronger and faster than ever. And that's not happening just because athletes care more than they used to or have more talent.

For athletes to discover their full potential, they need time to train. They need the best coaches available. Cutting-edge gear. Nutritionists to improve their diets. Even psychologists to focus their minds. In short, to be the very best, an athlete needs time, equipment, and expert help. And sport has evolved to provide these things...especially to male athletes.

But how about the women who see far fewer of these benefits? If the female athletes out there are already as good as they are now, how great could they be if they were supported just as men are? How great could they be if they were given the same time and resources?

UNLOCKING POTENTIAL

Let's go back to those stereotypes for a second. The ones that say women's bodies can't handle physical contact or can't be pushed as hard as men's. In this case, the stereotypes are a big reason women have had a difficult time proving doubters wrong. Women simply weren't allowed to attempt what men did. Which is a shame. Because as any athlete can tell you, until you train and try, you never know what your body is capable of. One of the best examples of this? Tennis's Serena Williams.

A LESSON FROM SERENA

The Williams sisters might be the greatest siblings in sport: Between the two of them, Serena and older sister Venus have won more than 50 Grand Slam singles and doubles titles. Tennis has been the center of their lives since they were little girls, training daily with their father. Serena started playing tennis when she was four. The dominance of the Williams sisters is no accident: Sure, they're physically gifted, but at every stage of their careers, they've worked hard.

And speaking of Serena, she's not just very good—in every sense, she's one of the most powerful women in sport. Tennis has never seen a woman with her raw strength. The oft No. 1-ranked American can serve a ball more than 128 mph (206 km/h). Good luck even seeing that serve, let alone returning it, in bounds, to a part of the court Serena can't reach. It's a serve that many male tennis stars envy.

There are many reasons Serena's serve moves at such velocity. First, her size helps. Serena is five foot nine and 150 pounds. Her relative height gives her better leverage on the ball than many of her shorter competitors. But height isn't everything—there are plenty of taller tennis players,

Serena Williams stretches to return a ball.

Mildred "Babe" Zaharias competing in the javelin, one of her many events.

including her older sister. Serena's major advantage is incredible strength and technique. Her muscular arms, back, core, and legs—combined with excellent movement—mean she can pummel that ball with a lot of force.

How did she achieve this level? One that saw her named *Sports Illustrated* Sportsperson of the Year in 2015? She was unquestionably born with more athletic talent than the average person. But to be *her* best, she still trained for decades with incredible focus, with the most experienced coaches, and, most importantly, refused to accept the idea that a woman couldn't—or shouldn't—be powerful. Serena Williams trained the way all male athletes have been training for ages. And the result makes people everywhere wonder just how powerful a woman can be.

When given the time and resources and expert help, in addition to the talent she was born with, Serena teaches us a lesson: that female athletes can be just as powerful as their male counterparts.

THE ORIGINAL POWERHOUSE: BABE

Mildred Didrikson Zaharias was her name, but everybody called her Babe. Born in 1911, Babe proved a girl could be a muscular athlete and dominate on every terrain. She was the first multi-sport female sports star the world had ever seen. Babe did it all: track and field, tennis, boxing, handball, billiards, golf, baseball, diving—you name it. Asked if there was anything she didn't play, Babe famously said, "Yeah, dolls."

Babe owned world records at a bunch of track and field events, and she won three Olympic medals. But her biggest love was golf. She was a founding member of the Ladies Professional Golf Association (LPGA), now one of the oldest and most successful pro women's sport associations on the planet. Babe was also the first woman to play on the men's golf circuit, the PGA Tour.

MORE THAN A PRETTY FACE

You've probably noticed: The world makes much of appearances. Just check out the magazine covers at the grocery store. Beautiful men and women are celebrated and lifted to celebrity status because of their looks. And it's no different in sport—beauty sells. But it especially sells in women's sports.

Though it's not the only reason women's tennis is one of the most successful sports out there, it's no secret that beautiful women help draw eyes to the game. Beauty is celebrated, but it can also lead to lazy and hurtful assumptions of why an otherwise talented athlete is getting opportunities. Even in sport, there's more to good looks than meets the eye.

THE PROS OF BEAUTY

Being attractive can lead to big benefits for an athlete. It can bring sponsorship opportunities and media coverage. It can even result in more fans.

Skylar Diggins is a WNBA All-Star who gets nearly as much attention for her looks as her on-court play. She is represented by the marketing company owned by Jay-Z. Nike sponsors Skylar, and her jersey is one of the top sellers in the WNBA. She has long black hair and a big smile…so, it's all because of her looks, right? It's not because she's a top-five scorer and one of the best young stars in the league?

Skylar says she'll take the attention her looks bring if it helps her sport. "As long as people take me seriously as an athlete, I don't really care why they watch us play," she says. "I'm just happy they're watching." For an athlete as gifted as Skylar—already one of the very best in her sport—her looks just add to her appeal. But it's important to note that they're not all that make her a star. Not even close.

IT'S NOT ALWAYS PRETTY

But on the other side of things, beautiful athletes can appear to face stronger criticism than others when they're anything but the very best. That criticism can be harsh, too. Former tennis star Anna Kournikova got a lot of heat for never winning a WTA singles title. Some said the blonde-haired Russian—who was also a model and dated pop stars—was "just a pretty face." It didn't seem to matter she was once ranked No. 8 in the world in singles…or that she was a World No. 1 doubles player and two-time Grand Slam winner. Her career was far better than the careers of most pro tennis players. You have to wonder: Would anyone have criticized her if she was less pretty?

In sports—and especially for women—good-looking people often have more to prove.

ABOVE: Skylar Diggins looks for a safe lane to pass through. MIDDLE: Anna Kournikova constantly dealt with a focus on her looks despite being a solid tennis pro. RIGHT: Australian tennis pro and U.S. Open champion Samantha Stosur.

MORE THAN JUST A STUNT

Sometimes, a woman's mere presence in sport can be viewed as a publicity stunt. When Canadian goaltender Shannon Szabados signed a contract with the Southern Professional Hockey League (SPHL) in 2014, some questioned her ability. Was this just a way to get more fans in the seats?

Well, Shannon put those questions to rest. She is the first woman to earn a shutout in men's pro hockey. Shannon and her Columbus Cottonmouths beat the Macon Mayhem 3–0 in December of 2015. She played in 25 games during the 2014–15 season, earned 15 wins, and even earned an assist—remember, Shannon is a goalie. Publicity stunt? Not so much. But is she ever popular. She even has her own Cottonmouths bobblehead doll!

Goalie Shannon Szabados holds her own with the men in an SPHL game.

DOUBLE STANDARDS

You would notice Alex Mack if you saw him walking down the street. Alex is six foot four, and he weighs 311 pounds. As much as a human being can resemble a tank, Alex does. And he puts his big frame to use: He's a center in the National Football League (NFL). Some would say he's built for football—his body is exceptional. Alex's job is to snap the ball and to protect his team's quarterback from other huge men on the opposing team. Alex is celebrated for his exceptional qualities: That he is a so-called freak of nature is a good thing.

Sadly, it's not always considered a good thing for a woman. Australian tennis player Samantha Stosur has one of the best serves on the women's tour. She also has some of the biggest biceps. Her muscles even have their own Twitter account. And while some celebrate her sculpted body—as they should—others express fear that she has bigger muscles than many men.

This is the double standard a woman faces: If she's muscular, she's manly. Or she's on steroids. Or she's unattractive. But the truth? Samantha is exceptional. Just like Alex, she's built for her sport.

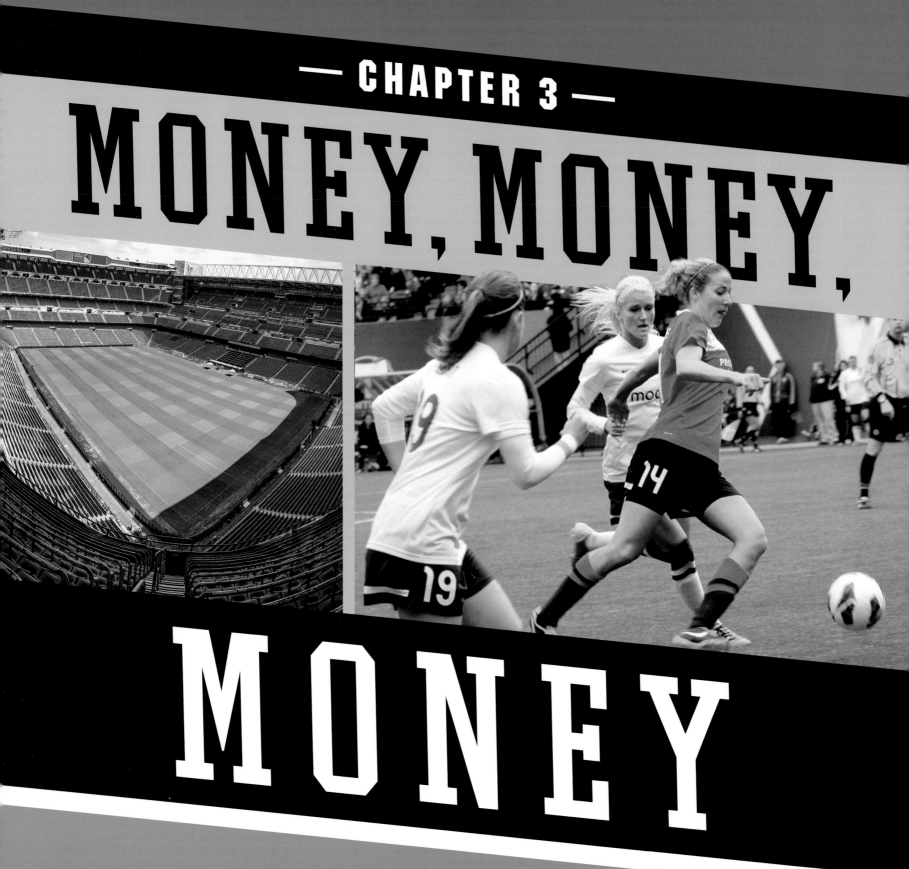

CHAPTER 3

MONEY, MONEY, MONEY

You know when something is so big that you can't describe it? Like that outdoor concert you went to with thousands of screaming people or maybe the time you saw Times Square in New York City? So, so big. Well, the money in pro sports is like that but...bigger. Some pro sports teams are worth more than three *billion* dollars. There are nine zeros in a billion.

So, how do these teams make all that money? Let's take the men's soccer club, Real Madrid C.F., as an example. Real's home stadium holds more than 85,000 fans, which equals more than 85,000 paying customers for every game. Really think about that for a second: If 1,000 kids go to your school, you'd have to find 84 more same-sized schools to fill that stadium. And you'd all have to pay to get in.

Ticket sales are just one piece of the financial pie. There are sponsorship deals from companies that pay to put their logos on a team uniform or on the playing surface. It's basically the same thing as when that local paint shop put its name on your midget soccer team's uniforms...except the number of dollars involved in professional sports is humongous. Then there are merchandise sales from team jerseys and T-shirts. And a ton of revenue from TV networks that pay huge dollars to broadcast games on their networks. In America, ESPN and Turner Sports signed a nine-year deal with the NBA that took effect in 2016. The cost to the TV network? Twenty-four billion dollars. Again, that's nine zeros.

What you probably noticed about all these big-dollar examples is that they involve men's sports. It is a very different story for women. Most women's pro sports generate only a fraction of what men's do. Some leagues lose money every year or fail altogether. In many instances, women's leagues don't sell out huge stadiums, their merchandise doesn't fly off shelves, and advertisers aren't banging down their doors for a chance to appear on a jersey, field, or court.

And that's among the main reasons we find such a glaring difference in salaries between men's and women's sports. Most female pro athletes make peanuts compared with their male counterparts. Even some of the best female athletes in certain pro sports need a second job just to be able to play. Imagine if your male teacher made double what your female teacher made for doing the same job. That sounds outrageous, but it's happening everywhere—in fact, in one NBA season, LeBron James's salary was more than *300 times* what Maya Moore's was to play in the WNBA.

The good news? Some women do make a very good living off their athletic abilities. For many, it's sponsorship dollars that pay the bills rather than their salaries. But more and more, women are speaking out for equal pay—like Carli Lloyd, Alex Morgan, Hope Solo, and other women's soccer stars filing an official wage complaint with U.S. soccer in March 2016. So it *is* possible as a woman to make a career out of kicking or dribbling a ball, sprinting down a field, crushing a drive down the 18th fairway, or smashing an ace. And it's more possible today than ever.

LEFT: Real Madrid's home stadium, Santiago Bernabéu.
RIGHT: Action in the National Women's Soccer League (NSWL).

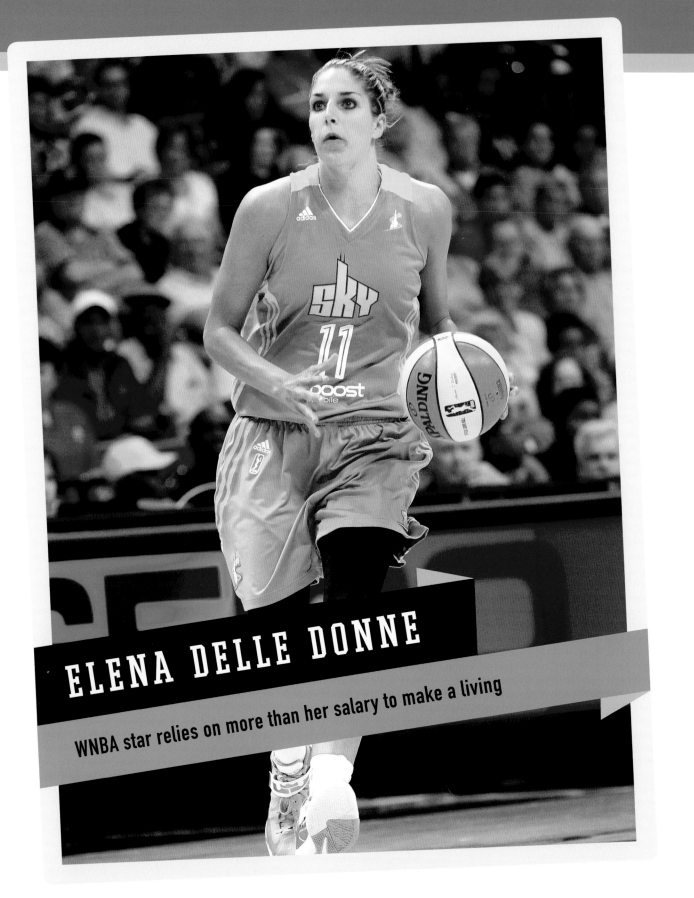

ELENA DELLE DONNE

WNBA star relies on more than her salary to make a living

Elena Delle Donne comes to a halt, 22 feet and 1¼ inches from the basketball rim. She takes flight and—swoosh!—the three-pointer drops. This is the first of many in her pro career. In her WNBA debut in 2013, Elena scores 22 points to lead the Chicago Sky to a win.

Elena is a six-foot-five guard from Delaware, and she's one of the best players in college history. It didn't take Elena long to become one of the best and most popular players in the WNBA, too. A couple of months into her rookie season, Elena earned more All-Star votes than any other player. That was a first for a rookie. Her reaction? "Shock," she says. "I had no idea I had that big of a following in the WNBA already."

It's that popularity, the result of a combination of talent (Elena was named league MVP in 2015), business savvy, and marketability, that has helped Elena make a career as a pro basketball player.

Q: WHAT'S THE BEST PART ABOUT YOUR JOB?

ELENA: I get paid to play the sport that I absolutely love. It doesn't feel like a job to me; it's incredible.

Q: HOW HAS THE EXPERIENCE BEEN, MAKING A LIVING AS A PRO BASKETBALL PLAYER?

ELENA: It's been going well for me. Obviously, being WNBA players, we don't make as much as the NBA players do, but I've been able to get sponsorship deals in addition to my shoe deal with Nike.

Q: DO YOU NEED TO BE A BUSINESSWOMAN AS WELL AS AN ATHLETE TO MAKE A LIVING?

ELENA: Definitely. I'm in the gym a lot, and I'm always working out and playing, but I also spend a lot of time in business meetings and speaking to CEOs and business minds about our league and ways to grow the game. And not only that, but other [sponsorship] avenues I can get involved in.

Q: A LOT OF WNBA PLAYERS PLAY IN RUSSIA OR TURKEY OR CHINA IN THE OFF-SEASON. HOW COME?

ELENA: The pay is huge—it's definitely hard to turn down that much money. It's a great time playing over there, and people are really into women's basketball. So a lot of my teammates love playing overseas. But basically, most people do it because the money is so big. A top-notch player who gets a multi-year deal could sign a million-dollar contract.

Q: HOW COME YOU DON'T PLAY OVERSEAS?

ELENA: Why in the world am I not doing that? (*Laughs*). I've always wanted to establish my brand here [to ensure sponsors and fans are familiar with me] and do other things that mean a lot to me. Family has always been so important. Another big reason to not go overseas is to keep my body healthy [and rest during the off-season]. And it's not always about money. It's about happiness.

Q: A LOT OF NBA PLAYERS MAKE MORE MONEY IN ONE SEASON THAN ALL THE PLAYERS IN THE WNBA COMBINED. IS THAT FRUSTRATING?

ELENA: It's disappointing. But you also have to keep in perspective that the NBA players are on TV all the time, there's a lot more people in the stands; they're going to make more money. I try not to compare the two because we are such a young league. If we continue to put a great product on the court, which we are, and players continue to get better, I think we can get to that level.

Q: WHERE DO YOU SEE THE WNBA IN 5 TO 10 YEARS?

ELENA: Hopefully we'll see more of the women in advertisements. When you see them on a Nike billboard, it's really special and it gets people excited about the game. I think we'll continue to see more fans in the seats. I definitely think we'll see more games on TV, which is so important. People just need to see us play in order to become fans.

UNDER-EXPOSURE

People just need to see us play. Elena touches on a near-universal problem with women's sport: a lack of exposure. The WNBA's Chicago Sky. The National Women's Soccer League's (NWSL) Portland Thorns FC. The Women's Chinese Basketball Association's (WCBA) Bayi China Telecom. Even if you know these teams exist, it's hard to be a fan of them if you can't watch their games. What reason *would* you have to be a fan unless you regularly heard about the teams or the players?

The fact is, we rarely do. Let's take the coverage of sports in the U.S., for example: Just 4 percent of U.S. sports media coverage is dedicated to women. A study of ESPN and its affiliated networks in the U.S. found the number was even lower: 1.5 percent of coverage is dedicated to female athletes. Whatever the number is, it's miniscule. Dr. Nancy Lough, the sports professor at UNLV who specializes in marketing, sponsorship, and women's issues, says the percentage of media coverage dedicated to women's sports has gone down in recent years, mainly because the percentage of men's sports coverage has gone up. "The bottom line is, if you want to be a fan of women's sport, you have to seek it out," Dr. Lough says. "Men's sport is constantly in your face. That's the big distinction."

ABOVE: Action in China's WCBA league. MIDDLE: Portland Thorns and Canadian National Team star Christine Sinclair (red jersey). RIGHT: Real Madrid's Cristiano Ronaldo, one of the world's richest athletes.

WHERE'S THE VALUE?

That big distinction also has a big effect on the amount of money generated by women's leagues. Because women's sports aren't "in your face," they don't represent as much value to a sponsor or an advertiser. Imagine you work for a candy company, and let's use the men's PGA Tour and the women's LPGA Tour as your potential markets. You want to promote your candy, so you want it to be seen by the most eyes. Consider this:

- Every PGA Tour event is televised and some tournaments draw more than 10 million viewers.

- Only select LPGA Tour events are televised, and even major tournaments draw fewer than 1 million viewers.

Now, if you're marketing that candy, you'll draw a lot more attention if you spend your money with the PGA Tour. It's more *marketable*.

What this all boils down to is a difficult predicament most female pro athletes face, because one challenge leads to many others. In the case of female athletes, since most of their games aren't on TV, the teams attract fewer sponsors, and they have less exposure. The result is that the league makes less money, and therefore the athletes are paid less.

MY, HOW IT'S GROWN

Exactly how much more money is tied up in pro sports today compared with in the past? Let's look at the evolution of prize money in golf. On the men's side, Billy Casper earned $25,000 when he won The Masters in 1970. Today's winner takes home more than $1.6 million—that's more than 60 times what Billy made. The women's game has leaped up significantly, too (though not by nearly as much). The LPGA Tour's total prize money is more than $61 million today, which is nearly 10 times as much as it was in 1970. One last tidbit on the big money in sports: In recent years, one of the highest-paid athletes in the world has been Portuguese soccer star Cristiano Ronaldo. He made $80 million *in a single year*. His salary accounted for 52 of those millions, and the remaining 28 came from endorsements. Cristiano's Spanish club team, Real Madrid C.F., signed him to a five-year deal through 2018, worth $206 million. It's safe to say he's set for retirement.

Let's take soccer, for example: The average salary in the U.S.-based NWSL is between $6,000 and $30,000 for a six-month season. A top-tier player on the men's pro side makes more than the high-end of that average—in a single week.

One reason for the disparity: You can find all the men's games on TV, so they attract sponsors and viewers and fans. But fewer than 10 percent of NWSL games were televised in 2015. It's hard to build a fan base—and it's hard to be a fan—when the games aren't on.

Like Elena said, the key to closing this gap is simple: *People just need to see us play.* When increased exposure leads to interest from advertisers, the amount of money involved can rise pretty quickly.

HIGH TO LOW

In 2007, Venus Williams once again hoisted Wimbledon's silver winner's plate over her head. It marked the fourth time in her career that the American won tennis's top prize (and she won it again the next year, too). There is no tennis tournament older or more prestigious than Wimbledon. But this 2007 win was historic for another reason—for the first time ever, Wimbledon awarded its female champ with the same amount of money as its male winner.

It was about time, too. Wimbledon was the last of tennis's four Grand Slam tournaments to give out equal prize money. The U.S. Open was the first, way back in 1970—Billie Jean King (remember her?) was a champion of that movement. And players like Venus are instrumental in continuing that fight.

TENNIS LEADS THE WAY

Some tournaments still award less to women, but equal prize money in many tournaments is among the main reasons tennis players are consistently the highest-paid women in pro sports. Of the 100 highest-paid athletes in the world in 2015, just two were women, and both of them wielded rackets and had killer serves. Maria Sharapova and Serena Williams each earned more than $20 million that year in prize money and endorsements. In fact, of the 10 highest-earning female athletes in the world that same year, 7 played tennis. Car racing, MMA (mixed martial arts), and golf rounded out the list.

And this brings us back to Elena's point about exposure: Tennis players are among the most recognizable faces in women's sports because we see them a lot. Their biggest tournaments are often held at the same time as the men's tournaments, and women get similar TV coverage. Because they're so visible to us, they're marketable, and they're signed to huge endorsement deals. Prior to testing positive for using a performance-enhancing drug in early 2016, Maria Sharapova had a banner 2015. She made $23 million in endorsements that year, had watches named after her, and even had her own line of Nike clothing. And in 2013, she founded a candy company called Sugarpova.

SHOW ME THE MONEY!

But unlike tennis, hockey is far less profitable. That's why top Finnish goalie and Olympic bronze medalist Noora Räty almost retired at age 25—because there wasn't a top women's league that could pay her enough to play. Though the Russian Women's Hockey League (RWHL) does pay its players, Noora didn't think the league was competitive enough. The North American–based CWHL is home to some of the best players in the world, but it offers no pay. "If I went there, I would have to get a job as well," Noora says. "I didn't want to play *and* have to work."

ABOVE: Venus Williams after 2007 Wimbledon win. MIDDLE: Finnish goalie Noora Räty. RIGHT: Danish tennis star Caroline Wozniacki.

But that's the reality for so many. If you look at any CWHL or NWSL roster, you will find a bunch of hockey and soccer players who double as supply teachers, physiotherapists, and personal trainers. They have second jobs—with flexible hours—so they can pay the bills and also be pro athletes.

It used to be this way for a lot of pro male athletes, too. (In fact, male players in some lesser-known leagues, like the National Lacrosse League [NLL], still need second jobs to pay the bills.) Back in the 1940s and 1950s, many athletes worked other jobs to supplement their income—some NHL players only earned $7,000 per season. The salaries for men are way higher today. You have to think, if there has been progress for men, there's hope for women, too.

And we're already seeing signs: The National Women's Hockey League (NWHL) of the U.S. had its inaugural season in 2015–2016 and paid a league minimum salary of $10,000. Kelli Stack of the Connecticut Whale was the NWHL's highest-paid player, earning $25,000. That's only half as much as the lowest-paid player makes in the men's American Hockey League (a league below the NHL). But it's a start.

As for Noora, she found her answer outside the women's game, in Mestis, a men's professional league in Finland, where she became the first female to record a shutout. She was paid more than she would have made in any pro women's league, enough for food and gas for her car and to set aside a little savings. "For a female player, it's big money," Noora says. Because, as she puts it, "You can make a career of hockey as a woman, but you probably won't get paid for it."

"Tennis as a sport is leading the way in gender equality. I think we will continue to see other sports level out as well, but I am proud to be a part of a sport that is taking this into consideration. It used to be hard to be a pro tennis player as a woman, but with everything leveling out, we now have the same opportunity to focus on our training and matches [as men]."

—Caroline Wozniacki

PACK UP AND GO

We find many of the world's most profitable and highest-profile sports leagues in one country: The United States of America. A little boy who grows up playing football dreams of starring in the NFL—because it's the best there is. The pay is astronomical, too. The U.S. is also home to the best leagues on offer for men's baseball, hockey, and basketball.

But this is less true for female athletes. As Elena explained, many of her fellow WNBA players go overseas in the off-season to play a second season. Consider that WNBA salaries range between $40,000 and $105,000 per year. Now consider this: The WNBA's Phoenix Mercury star Brittney Griner makes more than 10 times that during her off-season playing in the WCBA in China. About 70 percent of WNBA players also play in the WCBA or the Russian Women's Basketball Premier League or the Turkish Women's Basketball League (TKBL).

Similarly, many of the world's best female soccer players play in leagues like Damallsvenskan in Sweden and Women Bundesliga in Germany. These leagues offer year-long seasons, and the salaries are bigger than what women make playing five months of the year in the American-based NWSL.

So there are opportunities for bigger salaries out there for female pro athletes from North America...you just might have to pack up and move to find them.

WHAT GIVES?

The big question is this: Why are these women's pro leagues working in countries like China and Germany when the U.S. is so strong financially in other sports?

Part of the answer lies in the expansive sports landscape in North America. There is no shortage of professional sports organizations, which have been around so long they seem ingrained in the culture: MLB, NBA, NFL, NHL, PGA, and ATP (Association of Tennis Professionals). These are so high profile and have such loyal fan bases that they don't leave time for sports fans to take interest in much else. The market is what experts call "saturated"—it has no space for other things.

Now let's look back at countries like China and Sweden. There you'll find a fraction of the number of pro sports that capture the attention of their respective nations. Their markets are not saturated—they're more open to the possibilities offered by women's sport.

ABOVE: WNBA star Brittney Griner executes a block. MIDDLE: Sheryl Swoopes drives the lane for the Houston Comets of the WNBA. BOTTOM RIGHT: A joint game between Chinese and American basketball teams.

TRY, TRY, AND TRY...AGAIN

A lot of pro sports leagues—both men's and women's—have started up with great enthusiasm, only to fail. Some have failed miserably. You've probably never heard of a men's football league called the XFL, because it lasted only a single season in 2001 before folding. And there are dozens more just like it. All of them failed to find enough fans.

The Women's United Soccer Association (WUSA) has a short but expensive history. Founded in 2001, it folded in 2003 and lost about $100 million. The Women's Western Volleyball League ran from 1993 to 1994...and that was it. There were at least three attempts at a pro women's basketball league in the U.S. before the WNBA took root, too. Thankfully, that determination is finally paying off!

THE WNBA MODEL

One pro women's league that is working in the U.S. is the WNBA. This despite the fact that many believed it was doomed to fail when it was founded in 1996. Sheryl Swoopes, a three-time Olympic gold medalist and one of the best female players of all time, remembers it well. "A lot of people were saying, 'It's not gonna work, it's a professional women's league, they've tried this before,'" Sheryl says. Still, others felt the timing was right. The 1996 Olympics saw the American women's team capture the country's imagination and win gold. As Sheryl puts it, "People were hungry for more women's basketball." She was right, they were. The WNBA turns 20 in 2017.

But it has been far from easy. The league has survived financially only because it gets help from its partner, the NBA. In past seasons, the NBA spent more than $10 million annually to keep the WNBA going. The women's league is more self-sustaining these days, with some teams now reporting a profit.

If the WNBA teaches us anything, it's that a new league in North America benefits from help and promotion from a well-established partner. And it needs time to make a name for itself and to generate a fan base. It takes time and support (and maybe a bit of belief, too!)—only with these things can a fledgling league mature to the point where it can stand on its own two feet.

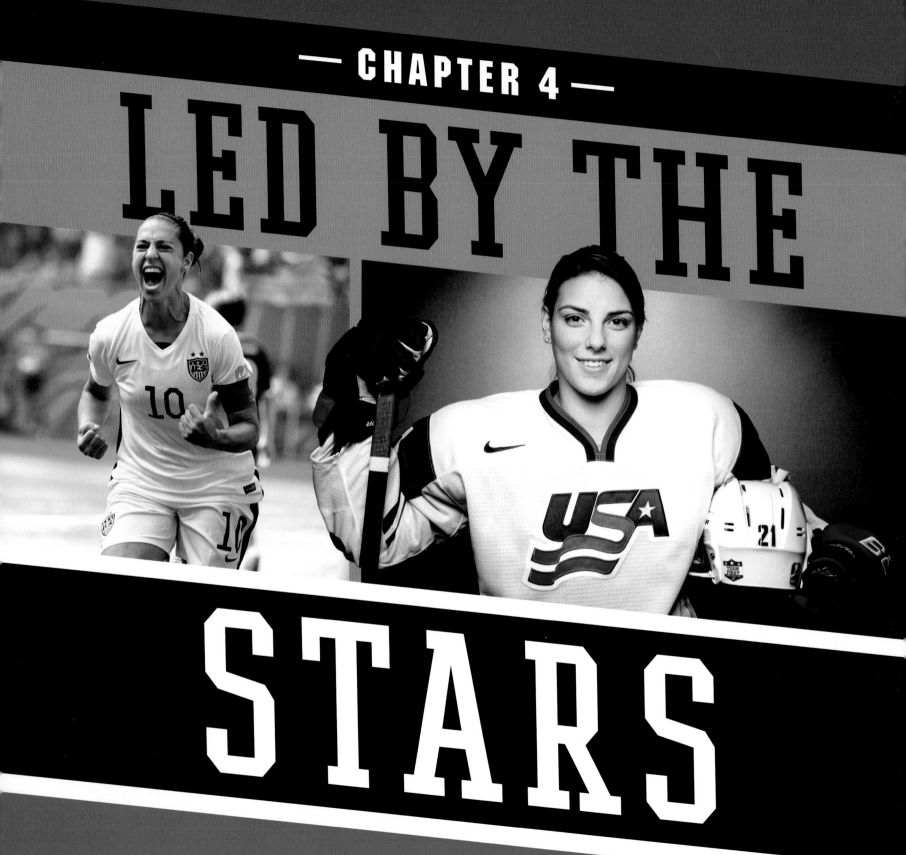

Hilary Knight is a big-game player—someone who *thrives* under pressure. Do you know anyone like that? It's almost as if the importance of the moment makes them perform better than they might otherwise.

At the 2015 Ice Hockey Women's World Championship in Sweden, Hilary did exactly that. The American forward scored seven goals and earned five assists in just five games. Hilary earned more points than any other player in the tournament. And not only that, but she led the American team to world championship gold.

Today in the U.S., registration in hockey among girls and women is at an all-time high. How come? Big-time events like that world championship and big-time players like Hilary.

You see, the result of a big game goes beyond the entertainment the players provide for the hundreds of thousands of fans who watch it. It goes beyond the medals won. A moment like that has a longer-lasting impact: These women are inspiring the next generation of female hockey players.

And that's what usually happens after big events like gold medal games and World Cups and major championships: Participation in that sport increases overall. This is vital to a sport's health. Because while professional leagues for women are important, their future depends on having more and more young girls deciding to try out sport.

It's a cycle that feeds itself. As there are more opportunities to see women compete on the biggest stages in sport, there are more girls and women who are inspired to play. That's one of the reasons, in many parts of the world, girls and women are now participating in sport like never before. They want to do the same thing themselves.

On the women's side, there is untold and unexplored potential. One reason for this is that the idea of women playing sports—professionally or recreationally—is relatively new in some places. Many countries are just starting to develop leagues and structures for girls. It's easy to grow when you're starting from nothing! That said, even the countries that are leaders in women's sport, like America, continue to experience growth in interest.

WNBA star Skylar Diggins needs to look no further than her hometown of South Bend, Indiana. In the late 1990s, when Skylar was a kid, there was only one competitive basketball team for girls there. "Now, it's multiple teams in my city," Skylar says. "It's so exciting to see all these girls playing and the sport becoming so popular, not just in the United States but around the world."

What drives this growth? Star athletes, big events, and, maybe most important of all, fun! Because once you start playing a game you love, who really wants to stop?

LEFT: U.S. Women's National Team soccer star Carli Lloyd.
RIGHT: U.S. hockey forward Hilary Knight.

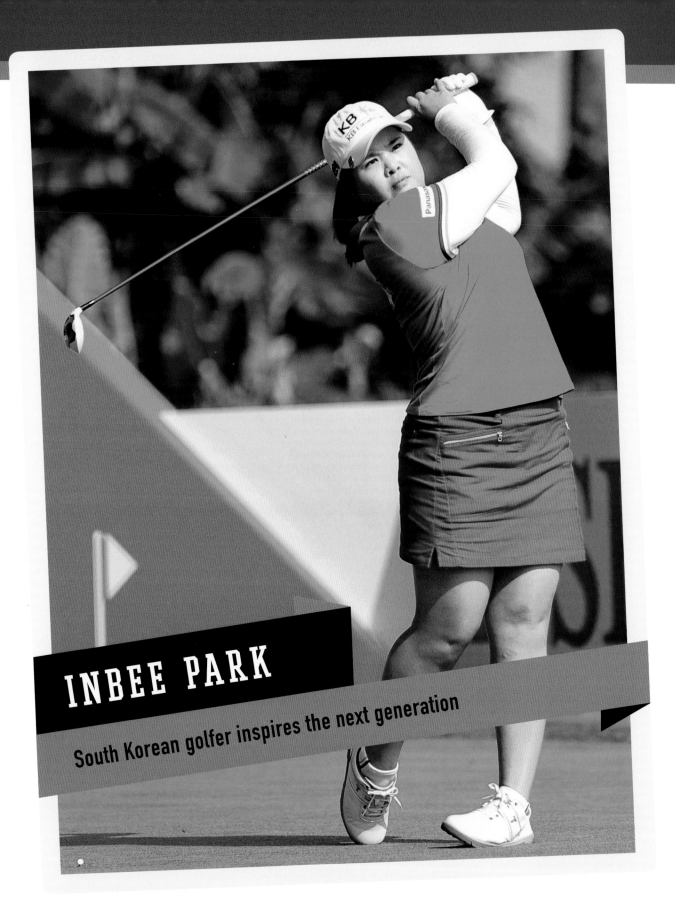

INBEE PARK

South Korean golfer inspires the next generation

Inbee Park taps in a short putt on the 18th hole at Sebonack Golf Club in New York and then throws her arms in the air while the crowd roars. Seconds later, she's doused in champagne by fellow LPGA Tour players, who spray the bubbly stuff all over Inbee. And for good reason, too: This is a historic moment.

A champagne-soaked Inbee poses for photos and TV cameras, holding that big silver U.S. Open trophy under her left arm. There's a massive smile on her face. Inbee's right hand is in the air, and she's holding up three fingers. How come? The South Korean golfer just won her third straight major championship of the season. The only other female golfer in history to do that is the late great Babe Zaharias.

Inbee has already made more than 12 million dollars in her career playing golf. She's the product of a growing game in South Korea and in the continent of Asia. And it's players like Inbee, owner of the World No. 1 ranking numerous times during her career, who are now inspiring more girls to get into the game.

Q: HOW HAVE YOU SEEN WOMEN'S GOLF CHANGE SINCE YOU JOINED THE LPGA TOUR?

INBEE: I started golf when I was 12. And what I see these days? I see 4-year-old girls on the range trying to hit the ball. Young and talented players will grow the game and make the LPGA Tour more competitive. The women's game keeps growing. All players have improved their game in all categories; they hit longer distances and have great short game skill.

Q: WHO DID YOU IDOLIZE IN THE GOLF WORLD WHEN YOU WERE A KID?

INBEE: Se Ri Pak was my idol when I was a young girl in Korea.

Q: YOU'VE HELD THE WORLD NO. 1 RANKING MANY TIMES. WHAT'S THAT LIKE?

INBEE: It is a dream. Like most professionals, I dream about being the world's best.

Q: YOU WERE THE YOUNGEST PLAYER TO WIN THE U.S. WOMEN'S OPEN AT AGE 19. THAT MUST HAVE PUT A LOT OF PRESSURE ON YOU AS A TEENAGER.

INBEE: It was lots of pressure after; I had all the attention. But I just keep focusing on my game as much as I can.

Q: WHAT IS LIFE LIKE FOR YOU WHEN YOU'RE BACK HOME IN SEOUL?

INBEE: When I come to the airport, I always get attention from media. And when I go outside my house, most people recognize me. I'm always excited to see them. In the U.S., sometimes people recognize me—especially when I go to the golf course.

Q: YOU'VE MADE A CAREER OUT OF YOUR SPORT, WHICH A LOT OF FEMALE ATHLETES CAN'T DO. DO YOU FEEL FORTUNATE, OR DO YOU FEEL IT'S YOUR RIGHT?

INBEE: It's half and half. My husband [coach Gi Hyeob Nam] and I worked very hard to be in this position. We also had a hard time, but we never gave up. I feel lucky that I have so many things now that I never ever imagined I would have.

Q: WHAT ADVICE WOULD YOU GIVE TO YOUNG KIDS ASPIRING TO PLAY GOLF PROFESSIONALLY?

INBEE: I always tell young players that they need to play other sports, too, and if they decide to play golf professionally, do not give up in any situation. You always get paid back at some point when you're trying hard. Never ever give up.

ATTENTION GRABBERS

Inbee watches four-year-old girls work on their swings on the driving range, something she never saw when she was little. Plenty of numbers back up the change she's seeing: Golf has exploded among girls and women in her lifetime, and Asia is at the center of the boom.

That growth and surge in interest is also having a big effect on the LPGA Tour, where Inbee plays: Countries like Thailand, Singapore, Japan, China, and Taiwan all host pro tournaments of their own now.

THE SE RI PAK EFFECT

Inbee remembers the moment she was inspired to make golf her career. She was nine years old and asleep. Awoken by her screaming parents, Inbee ran to see what the commotion was about. That's when she saw her parents celebrating in front of the TV as they watched fellow South Korean Se Ri Pak win the U.S. Open. That was back in 1998.

Maybe you've heard of Tiger Woods. Well, he and Se Ri had a similar effect on golf: They brought more people and fans to the game.

Inbee is a firsthand example of Se Ri's impact. Three years after Inbee watched that U.S. Open celebration, she moved to Florida to pursue golf. She was 12 years old.

LEFT: South Korean golfer Se Ri Pak. MIDDLE LEFT: Italian figure skater Carolina Kostner. MIDDLE RIGHT: Iraqi sprinter Ala'a Hikmat. FAR RIGHT: Steffi Graf hoists the U.S. Open trophy in 1995.

SHOOT FOR THE STARS

Let's take a look at a few other athletes who have helped put sport on the map in their home countries:

- Sheryl Swoopes: Nobody did more for women's basketball in the early days of the WNBA than this player. The three-time league MVP not only drew comparisons to Michael Jordan (and yes, she loved that), but she was also the first female player to have a basketball shoe named after her. Little girls not only wanted to play like Sheryl, they also wanted to wear her Nike Air Swoopes. "That was so, so cool," Sheryl says. "For Nike to make me the first [woman] to have my own basketball shoe, it was amazing."

- Carolina Kostner: This Italian essentially introduced her nation to figure skating. At the 2006 Olympics in Turin, Italy, she captured the attention of the population with a sport that wasn't well known there. It was Carolina who carried the Italian flag at the Opening Ceremony. "The whole nation was curious about what I was going to do, about my sport," she says. And so they tuned in like never before. Figure skating was the most-watched event on TV in Italy during the Olympics. "I was kind of the ambassador for the future," Carolina says.

- Ala'a Hikmat: This Iraqi sprinter was the lone female to represent her country at the 2004 Olympics. This was enormous because the country had experienced a tremendous amount of violence, and Iraqi women had

STEFFI'S INFLUENCE

Caroline Wozniacki grew up idolizing German tennis legend Steffi Graf. Steffi is a legend: She won an incredible 22 Grand Slam tournaments, and she is the only person in history to win all four singles Grand Slam titles and the Olympic gold medal in one year. That's called a Golden Slam.

"Steffi was not only an amazing player but such a good role model on and off the court as well," Caroline says. **"She showed so much passion for the sport."**

not been competing in sport for years. With so many eyes on the Olympics, Ala'a encouraged a renewed interest in sport among other women in her home country. By the 2012 Summer Olympics, three Iraqi women competed at the Games.

• Caroline Wozniacki: Interest in tennis in Denmark is surging thanks in part to Caroline's success as a former World No. 1. There weren't many players in Denmark turning pro when she was little. It's her goal to help change that. "Tennis in Denmark is continually growing, and I couldn't be more proud," she says. "I hope I can make an impact on the younger players and give them the opportunity to play at higher levels and make Denmark a more influential country in tennis."

• And in the future? The U.S. alone is home to a countless number of the world's most famous female athletes. Check out how that's contributing to participation rates in the country: During the 1994–95 school year, 2.24 million girls played a sport in high school. By 2013–14, participation had skyrocketed to 3.26 million. In a decade, the number increased by more than a million. And it's still growing.

THE PENALTY KICK HEARD AROUND THE WORLD

None of these women would have had a chance to inspire the next generation of athletes were it not for the big events that allowed them to showcase their talent. In recent history, one of the most impactful events happened on the soccer field: the 1999 Women's World Cup.

And at the center of it was a muscular, blonde American named Brandi Chastain.

"IT WAS CHAOS"

Brandi waits for the referee to blow the whistle, the signal that she can take her penalty kick. The whistle goes and the crowd of 90,185 at the Rose Bowl falls silent. Brandi takes a deep breath: Make this shot, and Team USA beats China to wins the World Cup. She gets a running start and hits that ball, left-footed. *Bam*—it's in the net.

She drops to her knees, rips off her white USA jersey, and waves it over her head while the crowd roars. Her ripped abs and her celebration remain one of the most famous moments in sports history. "It was chaos," Brandi says today. "Every possible emotion takes over. Exponentially. By a million."

THE AFTEREFFECTS

That World Cup's display of women's soccer affected the entire world's view of the sport. The inaugural Women's World Cup in 1991 wasn't even on TV.

But in 1999, all 32 games were televised, stadiums were packed, and in the weeks that followed, the American women graced the covers of *Time*, *Sports Illustrated*, and *People*. No women's sporting event had ever struck such a chord or touched such a wide audience.

LEFT: U.S. Women's National Team's Brandi Chastain celebrates her 1999 Women's World Cup–winning goal. RIGHT: Team USA celebrates winning the 2015 Women's World Cup.

WOMEN'S SOCCER BY THE NUMBERS

In 1971, three national women's soccer teams played a total of two matches. By 2010, 141 national teams played more than 500 matches in all international competitions. There are now more than 170 national women's soccer teams in the world. And more than 26 million girls play soccer on registered teams worldwide, with the U.S. and Germany leading the way. This growth wasn't unexpected, however. Back in 1995, Sepp Blatter, the president of FIFA, told the world: "The future of football is feminine."

As Bill Clinton, America's president at the time, said: "It's going to have a bigger impact than people ever realized, and it will have a far-reaching impact not only in the United States but also in other countries."

We are still seeing those effects today—female soccer players around the world have improved significantly since 1999. Consider this: Japan didn't register a shot against the U.S. team in a tune-up for the Women's World Cup in 1999, but it won the whole tournament in 2011. In 1991, Costa Rica wasn't even on the radar, but by 2015 it qualified for its first-ever World Cup. And America is now producing stars like Carli Lloyd, who scored three times—three times!—in a 2015 World Cup final that again captured the country's hearts.

There are more fans of the women's game today than ever, too. More than 20 million Americans watched the 2015 Women's World Cup final between the U.S. and Japan. It's the most-watched U.S. soccer game in history—for women and men. It drew more viewers than the 2014 World Series and the 2015 NBA finals. And that 1999 World Cup, with Brandi's big moment, was the kick-starter.

"Gosh, isn't sport awesome?" Brandi says. "That you can have a chance to contribute in a way that helps your team win and has such an impact. It brought attention to the game on a wider scale. That gives me chills."

CHAPTER 5

THE

FUTURE

In 2014, a 13-year-old girl with a 70-miles-per-hour fastball and a wicked stare from the mound captured the world's imagination. Her name was Mo'ne Davis.

The star pitcher for the Taney Dragons from South Philadelphia led her team to the Little League Baseball World Series (LLBWS) final. She was the 18th girl in history to compete in the tournament for youth, ages 12 and 13, and the first girl to pitch a shutout.

After that baseball tournament, Mo'ne was *everywhere*. She threw the ceremonial first pitch at a World Series game. She wrote a memoir. She was on the cover of *Sports Illustrated*. She even appeared in a documentary by award-winning director Spike Lee. And as Mo'ne herself put it—with that perfect stare—"I throw 70 miles per hour. *That's* throwing like a girl."

The best part of Mo'ne's story is this: We're going to see more and more young girls like her. We're going to see more and more talented female athletes empowered and motivated and given opportunities that girls before them simply never had. And we're going to see more girls pushing the boundaries of what many thought possible.

For if there is one thing all athletes agree on—no matter what sport they play, where they come from, or what their age or sex—it's that the future of women's sport looks good. There is still a lot of work to do. But female athletes are working hard to promote and grow their sport simply by doing what they do on a field of play. And they double as ambassadors.

Of course, so do male athletes. But what is unique to women's sport is that its athletes feel a greater responsibility to their roles as ambassadors. Male leagues like the NBA and NHL are already established, stable, and raking in money. Their female counterparts are still growing. And so their players are further invested in helping these leagues flourish.

Tulsa Shock star Skylar Diggins considers promoting the WNBA a part of her job. "I endorse it, and I carry it with me wherever I go," Skylar says. "The players before me have done a lot, and we're still making strides now to give people something to aspire to and give young girls a bar to strive for."

Thanks to athletes like Mo'ne and Skylar, that bar is getting higher and higher.

LEFT: Mo'ne Davis pitches in the Little League World Series.
RIGHT: Tulsa Shock star guard Skylar Diggins.

CHRISTEN PRESS

American soccer star believes sport can make a difference

A Scottish defender heads a ball out of her goalie's crease, away from the encroaching American forward. But it lands right at the feet of U.S. midfielder Christen Press. She controls it quickly in the penalty arc, about 65 feet (20 meters) from the goal. That's probably double the distance between your teacher and the back of your classroom. Then Christen does what Christen does best: She propels a rocket past the diving Scottish goaltender. The 18,656 fans in Jacksonville, Florida, roar as Christen throws her hands in the air, jumping and grinning as her teammates hug her.

Remember the biggest goal of your life? Or when you got a standing ovation for your performance in the school play? This is that moment for Christen. It's the first goal of her career on the national team. And most impressively of all, it comes just 13 minutes into her first-ever game. Christen isn't finished, though. Nineteen minutes later, she strikes again. Before this game, only two American women had scored twice in their national team debuts. Christen makes it three.

Q: THE U.S. WOMEN'S NATIONAL TEAM IS CONSISTENTLY AMONG THE WORLD'S BEST. WHY IS THAT?

CHRISTEN: We have so many women playing soccer in this country and a college system that heavily promotes young players. That in itself, the cultural aspect, the women's rights, the support from our federation, gives us such an advantage and such a depth that other teams aren't necessarily getting at this stage in the women's game. The facilities that we have access to, the resources that they [the U.S. Women's National Team] put at our fingertips, it means when players come into the national team, they take off.

Q: WHAT'S THE MOST DIFFICULT PART OF YOUR JOB?

CHRISTEN: The travel, definitely. It's a hard life that we have. We spend 200 days out of the year in a hotel, on the road [to play the top competition from around the world]. Because of that we have to sacrifice a lot. But I think we all do that for something much bigger than simply winning a tournament.

Q: THE WORLD CUP AND THE OLYMPICS GIVE US A SHOWCASE OF THE BEST WOMEN SOCCER PLAYERS ON THE PLANET. WHAT ABOUT THE YEARS BETWEEN?

CHRISTEN: I sort of feel like everything we do in off years is in the shadows; there's always bigger sporting events, there's always something else going on [in those off years]. It's the nature of international women's soccer: Twice in every four-year cycle, we have a moment where the spotlight's on us and all the pressure's on us, and it's time. But the years we don't have major events, we're playing and training just as hard in our respective leagues.

Q: TO WHAT EXTENT DO YOU SEE YOURSELF AS AN AMBASSADOR FOR THE WOMEN'S GAME?

CHRISTEN: This is so much more than just the entertainment business, it's so much more than just a game. I think the U.S. national team specifically has such an opportunity to grow the game and build a legacy that's lasting. We've had a lot of success in the past, and it's driven the sport as a whole. You can see in our country, the amount of support that we get, the amount of interest that the game sparks. I think we have a really unique opportunity to do something great for the sport and for all the people that come after us. That's why it's so important to win, that's why it's so important for us to be at the top of our game, because we have so much power in our sport to make a difference, to make a change. And it goes beyond just women's soccer and young girls playing soccer. It's women in sports in general, because there's a long way that we need to go still.

BORDER-TO-BORDER DIFFERENCES

Christen points out the cultural advantage Team USA has, and she's right. Along with countries like Japan, Sweden, and Australia, America is improving at valuing female athletes. These nations increasingly respect their women and girls playing sports.

In some countries, it's a very different story. In some Middle Eastern nations, such as Iran and Saudi Arabia, women have been banned from even entering stadiums during pro sports competitions. That might be unimaginable to you. But these countries are worlds apart from the West when it comes to women's rights. Consider this: In Saudi Arabia, women weren't allowed to vote in an election until 2015.

This is discrimination based on cultural reasons, religious interpretations, and a deep-rooted belief that women aren't equal to men. So while it's true that there is discrimination in the U.S. surrounding a woman fighting in the Ultimate Fighting Championship (UFC) or one with "manly" muscles, in Iran, a woman can be charged with spreading propaganda against the country's government...all because she wants to *watch* a game in a stadium.

THE RIGHT TO PLAY

Actually playing sport is another challenge. Men and women in some countries are fighting to allow women to participate, and three nations, Saudi Arabia, Qatar, and Brunei, just sent their first-ever female participants to the London 2012 Summer Olympics. Think about that: 112 years after women started competing at the Olympics, these three countries sent their first. (Mind you, Saudi Arabia sent women to compete only because the International Olympic Committee [IOC] threatened to ban the nation from the Games if it didn't.)

"You have to be patient," says Dr. Nancy Lough, the UNLV professor whose areas of expertise includes gender equity and women's leadership in sport. "You have to understand that we're talking about societal change, social change—and those things don't happen quickly."

LEFT: A woman protests the jailing of Ghoncheh Ghavami, an Iranian who fought for a woman's right to attend public sporting events.
TOP RIGHT: Saudi Arabia's Sarah Attar in London in 2012. FAR RIGHT: Qatar's Nada Arkani trains for the Olympics.

Women's sport has come a long way, yes, but as Christen and Dr. Lough have pointed out, there is a long, long way to go. It's going to take time. And that's because social change isn't easy. Getting people to alter widely held beliefs and challenging what they've been used to isn't easy. Consider what has happened in the U.S. with gay marriage: It was a major issue for over two decades before it was legalized in June 2015. Change takes time indeed.

YOUNG LEAGUES

Speaking of time, here is something to consider when we look at the future of women's pro sports: The majority of the leagues in existence today are very young. Most are fewer than 20 years old, and some are fewer than 5. On the men's side, Major League Baseball (MLB) has been around since 1869. It's an institution. There is no major women's sports league even close to that old. The NBA was founded in 1946. The WNBA didn't come along until more than 50 years after that.

And women's pro leagues for sports like soccer, hockey, and basketball in countries like Sweden, Switzerland, Russia, and China are even younger than the WNBA. They're newcomers. There's a reason two of the most popular women's sports organizations out there—the WTA (founded in 1973) and the LPGA Tour (1950)—are also among the oldest. Success, just like social change, doesn't happen overnight.

LEADERS OF THE PACK

In sports, there are still a few more areas where a strong female presence has yet to be established. Take a look at the person pacing the sidelines or standing behind the bench, yelling instruction to the players: the coach. It remains the exception—not the rule—to see a female in that role.

CALLING ALL COACHES...

In North America, for example, men coach more than half of all women's teams. At the professional level, there are even fewer female coaches. Of the nine teams in the NWSL to start the 2015 season, Laura Harvey was the only woman in a head coach position. Laura also won the NWSL's Coach of the Year award in 2014 and 2015.

If a man can coach a bunch of women, why can't a woman coach a bunch of men? She can, of course. But rarely is she hired for the role. And since so few women are in these positions, few even dream of taking on these jobs. More women need to push for these jobs. Because as it stands, female coaches are nearly nonexistent in men's pro leagues.

YOU CAN CALL HER "COACH"

You currently won't find a female coach behind the bench in major leagues like the NHL or MLB…yet. But in 2014, the San Antonio Spurs hired the first full-time female assistant coach in NBA history, adding former WNBA star Becky Hammon to its staff. That decision was historic, making the NBA among the most forward-thinking leagues in this regard. Meanwhile in Scotland, Wimbledon champion Andy Murray sought out the coaching expertise of two-time major champion and former WTA star Amélie Mauresmo. Then in January of 2016, the NFL's Buffalo Bills hired Kathryn Smith as an assistant coach—the first ever full-time female coach in the league's history.

BOTTOM LEFT: NWSL coach Laura Harvey during her time on the staff at London's Arsenal club. TOP LEFT: Becky Hammon drives the basket in the WNBA. TOP MIDDLE: NBPA executive director Michele Roberts. TOP RIGHT: MLB's senior VP of baseball operations, Kim Ng.

MALE-DOMINATED OFFICES

The look in the front office is no different from that at the sidelines. The front office is where those who run the team work. And a pro team's offices are full of men in suits. Rarely is a woman in sight.

One of the most important roles behind the scenes is that of the general manager (GM). The GM decides on player trades and contracts and usually determines the coaching staff. It's the GM who's responsible for building the team. And no major North American–based men's sports team has *ever* hired a female to do that job.

On the other side, plenty of female pro sports organizations have entrusted this job to a man. For example, more than half the GMs in the NWSL in 2015 were men.

But why is that? It happens for a lot of reasons. Among them, the fact that many women don't consider these jobs a possibility because they don't see women in these roles in the first place. Whereas men have held these positions for years.

EXECUTIVE TRAILBLAZERS

That said, women are breaking into these executive positions, even if it's happening slowly. A couple of examples:

- Kathy Carter: The president of Soccer United Marketing (SUM), she is in charge of selling Major League Soccer (MLS) to the public—a big role for a league that is still young and looking to build its fan base.

- Michele A. Roberts: In 2014 she was hired as executive director of the National Basketball Players Association (NBPA), the union that represents NBA players. She's the first woman to lead a major men's pro sports union in North America.

- Kim Ng: MLB's senior vice president for baseball operations, she was also the first woman ever interviewed for a GM role in MLB.

So, though few and far between, women are making their way into those front offices. And the more women we see there, the more they'll inspire others to aspire to those ranks. Sometimes you just need to see something to believe it's possible, right? These women are living proof.

The hope is that one day, the accomplishments of women in sport—in boardrooms, in coaching roles, in the front office—won't be unique. That a woman promoted to a position of power in a pro men's sports franchise won't be the first. The hope is she'll be one of many.

CONCLUSION

There is no question: Men and women live in different worlds when it comes to professional sports.

There is less TV coverage for women athletes, lower salaries to do the same job, and few women in front office positions. In other facets of life, too, there exists great inequality: Discrimination based on gender in some countries means women can't even leave their homes without a man accompanying them. It's easy to be pessimistic when we see all that.

But it's important to remember, when it comes to sport, that the value of competition isn't always monetary. It isn't always in the form of media coverage or attention.

Most of us will never play in a game as big as the World Cup final or inspire a generation of kids to become soccer players. But there are plenty of other benefits we can enjoy, no matter how big or small the game is. If you play high school sports, you're less likely to drop out of school than someone who doesn't play. You're more likely to go to college or university. You're less likely to be obese or to develop weak bones. Plus, it's a heck of a lot of fun. Not bad!

Whether you're a fan of tennis or golf or baseball or no sport at all, it's about more than a game. Billie Jean King turned a tennis match into a battleground for women's rights. Women in Iran are doing the same today in their protest to gain entry into stadiums to watch live games. Sport is a way to make a statement. It doesn't have to make you rich and famous.

But women are going to get paid and recognized more for their athletic talent in the future. The progress is going to continue. I see it firsthand: I grew up playing hockey, which is nearly a prerequisite where I'm from (Canada), and especially if your family values sports and activity (and tiring out over-energized kids), like mine does. Fewer than a couple decades have passed since I graduated high school, and in that time, the amount of change I've seen is incredible. I coach a high school girls' team in the Toronto area, and every player on the team plays at a high level. That wasn't the case when I was a kid. It's no longer a novelty to be a hockey-playing girl. These girls play for teams that didn't exist when I was little. (And I'm not *that* old.)

I cover sports for a living. I attended the Olympics in London in 2012, and the biggest star there was a multi-sport athlete named Jessica Ennis. When she won gold in heptathlon, it felt like the stadium might burst. People even wore cardboard masks of her face over their own faces. It didn't matter that they could hardly see through the tiny eyeholes. Jessica was as celebrated as any athlete at those Olympics. She was the biggest thing in sport. And rightly so.

Seeing things like this, the growth of women's hockey in Canada and Jessica dominating the world's biggest celebration of athleticism, makes me excited. It makes me optimistic about the future. I hope you are, too.

British Olympian Jessica Ennis competes in Manchester.

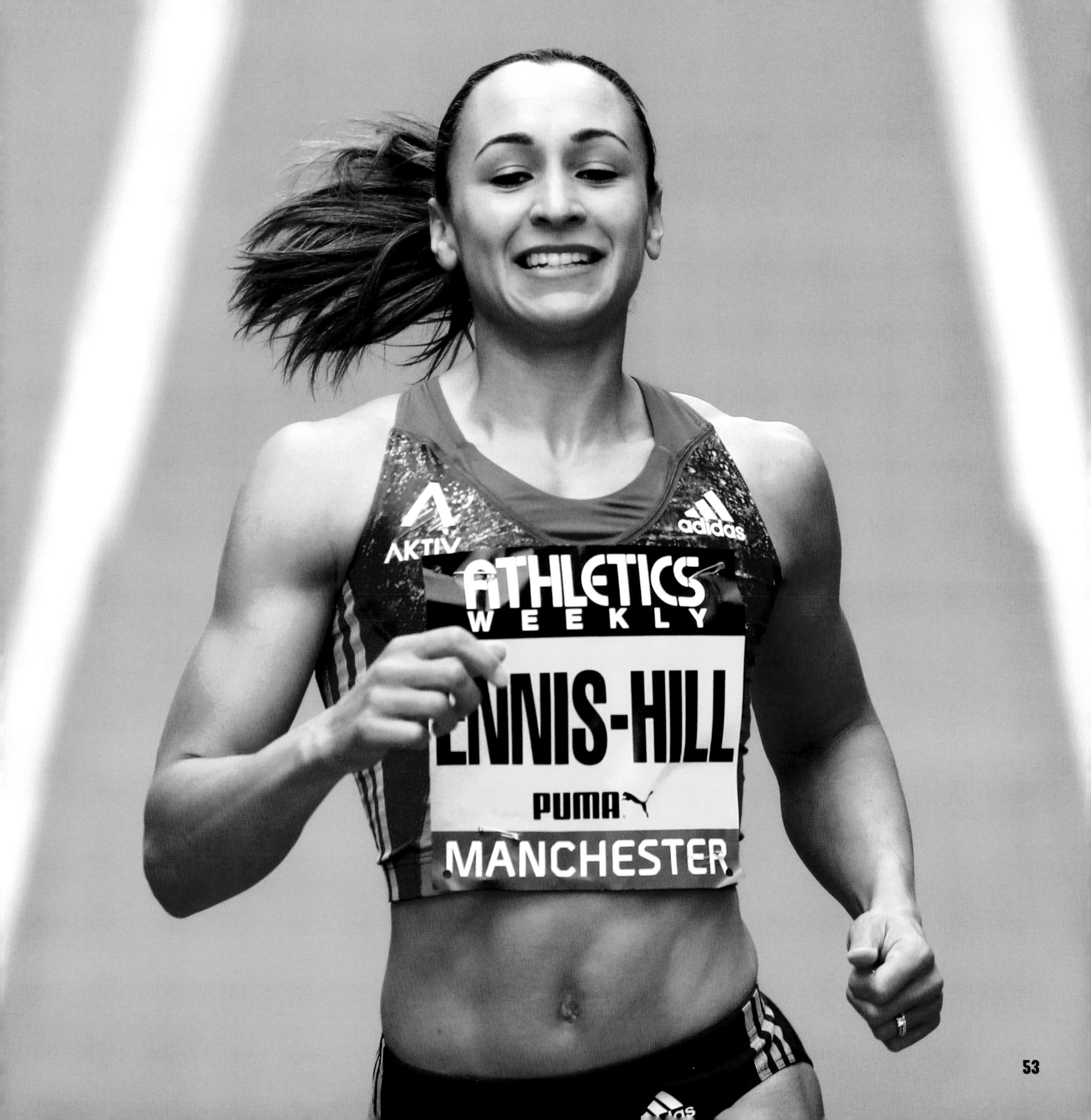
AKTIV
adidas
ATHLETICS
WEEKLY
NNIS-HILL
PUMA
MANCHESTER

INDEX

SOURCES

Associated Press. "A Triumph for Women from Qatar, Saudi Arabia and Brunei." *The New York Times*, Aug. 3, 2012. http://www.nytimes.com/2012/08/04/sports/olympics/for-women-from-qatar-saudi-arabia-and-brunei-a-simple-triumph.html?_r=0.

Campbell, Morgan. "Sportonomics: Can Women's Sports Level the Commercial Playing Field?" *The Toronto Star*, August 11, 2014.

Caple, Jim. "Will Kim Ng Be MLB's First Female GM?" ESPN.com, September 26, 2015. http://espn.go.com/espnw/news-commentary/article/13371785/will-kim-ng-mlb-first-female-gm.

Cooky, Cheryl and Michael A. Messner. *Gender in Televised Sports.* Los Angeles: Center for Feminist Research, University of Southern California, June 2010.

Druzin, Randi. *The Complete Idiot's Guide to Women in Sports.* New York: Alpha Books, 2001.

Federation International de Football Association. *265 Million Playing Football*, 2007. http://www.fifa.com/mm/document/fifafacts/bcoffsurv/emaga_9384_10704.pdf.

Guttmann, Allen. *Women's Sports: A History.* New York: Columbia University Press, 1991.

Lisi, Clemente A. *The U.S. Women's Soccer Team: An American Success Story.* Lanham, MD: Rowan and Littlefield Publishers, Inc., 2013.

Jaafari, Shirin. "Iranian Women Fight for the Right to Attend Sports Events in their Country." Public Radio International, July 7, 2014. http://www.pri.org/stories/2014-07-07/iranian-women-fight-right-attend-sports-events-their-country

Madhani, Aamer. "Iraq's Solo Female Athlete in Olympics Has Already Won." *Chicago Tribune*, July 16, 2004. http://articles.chicagotribune.com/2004-07-16/news/0407160227_1_iraqi-olympic-committee-iraqi-officials-athletes.

Margolis, Jason. "The Struggle for Female Soccer Equality in Brazil." Public Radio International, May 2013. http://www.pri.org/stories/2013-05-27/struggle-female-soccer-equality-brazil.

National Federation of State High School Federations. *2014–2015 High School Participation Survey Results.* http://www.nfhs.org/ParticipationStatics/PDF/2014-15_Participation_Survey_Results.pdf.

Renzetti, Elizabeth. "Unforced Error: Where Are the Female Athletes on TV?" *The Globe and Mail*, July 7, 2014.

Sandomir, Richard. "Women's World Cup Final Was Most-Watched Soccer Game in United States History." *New York Times*, July 6, 2015.

Stevenson, Betsey. "Title IX and the Evolution of High School Sports." NBER Working Paper Series, The Wharton School, University of Pennsylvania, October 2007. http://wsb.wharton.upenn.edu/documents/research/TitleIXandtheEvolutionofHighSchooSports-11-07.pdf.

Ware, Susan. *Game, Set, Match: Billie Jean King and the Revolution in Women's Sports.* Chapel Hill, NC: The University of North Carolina Press, 2011.

Weinberg, Rick. "Kerri Strug Fights Off Pain, Helps U.S. Win Gold." ESPN.com, July 19, 2004. http://espn.go.com/espn/espn25/story?page=moments/51.

Women's Sports Foundation. "History of Title IX." http://www.womenssportsfoundation.org/home/advocate/title-ix-and-issues/history-of-title-ix/history-of-title-ix.

"The World's Highest-Paid Athletes." *Forbes*, 2014. http://www.forbes.com/pictures/giig45jli/1-floyd-mayweather/.

Ibid., 2015. http://www.forbes.com/athletes/.

Interviews

Campbell, Cassie
Chastain, Brandi
Donne, Elena Delle
Diggins, Skylar
Kostner, Carolina
Lough, Dr. Nancy
Park, Inbee
Parsons, Norm
Patrick, Danica
Press, Christen
Räty, Noora.
Swoopes, Sheryl
Tate, Miesha
Wozniacki, Caroline

ACKNOWLEDGMENTS

I have never written a book, let alone written for kids, before. Thank you to John Crossingham for trusting me with a topic you're so passionate about, and for everything you taught me throughout the process. Mike Adach, you're a gem. Thank you. D, only an eagle eye catches a double space. Thanks to P and D. And most importantly, to the women who wanted to take part in this book—to Cassie and Elena and Sheryl and Skylar and Inbee and Christen and Miesha and the list goes on—thank you all for sharing your stories.

—Kristina